FASHION FIGURES

MARY-KATE & ASHLEY OLSEN

CHIC

HIGH-FASHION DESIGNERS

Jessica Rusick

Checkerboard Library

An Imprint of Abdo Publishing
abdobooks.com

abdobooks.com

Published by Abdo Publishing, a division of ABDO, PO Box 398166, Minneapolis, Minnesota 55439.
Copyright © 2020 by Abdo Consulting Group, Inc. International copyrights reserved in all countries.
No part of this book may be reproduced in any form without written permission from the publisher.
Checkerboard Library™ is a trademark and logo of Abdo Publishing.

Printed in the United States of America, North Mankato, Minnesota
052019
092019

THIS BOOK CONTAINS
RECYCLED MATERIALS

Design: Aruna Rangarajan, Mighty Media, Inc.
Production: Mighty Media, Inc.
Editor: Rebecca Felix
Design Elements: Shutterstock Images
Cover Photograph: AP Images
Interior Photographs: AP Images, pp. 5, 13, 21; Everett Collection NYC, pp. 7, 9; Getty Images, pp. 19, 23; Shutterstock Images, pp. 11, 15, 17, 25, 27, 28 (left, middle, right), 29 (left, right)

Library of Congress Control Number: 2018966465

Publisher's Cataloging-in-Publication Data

Names: Rusick, Jessica, author.
Title: Mary-Kate & Ashley Olsen: chic, high-fashion designers / by Jessica Rusick
Other title: Chic, high-fashion designers
Description: Minneapolis, Minnesota :Abdo Publishing, 2020 | Series: Fashion figures | Includes online
    resources and index.
Identifiers: ISBN 9781532119538 (lib. bdg.) | ISBN 9781532173998 (ebook)
Subjects: LCSH: Olsen, Ashley, 1986- --Juvenile literature. | Olsen, Mary-Kate, 1986---Juvenile literature. |
    Fashion designers--United States--Biography--Juvenile literature. | Women actors- Biography--Juvenile
    literature. | Women entrepreneurs--Biography--Juvenile literature.
Classification: DDC 921 [B]--dc23

CONTENTS

TALENTED TWINS

Mary-Kate and Ashley Olsen are twin sisters and child stars who became high-end fashion designers. Their designs are inspired by comfortable fit and luxury fabrics. The Olsens are known for their simple, elegant, well-made clothing.

The Olsens have been in the spotlight since they were babies. They became beloved child actors starring in the TV show *Full House*. Olsen twins products dominated the **tween** market. There were movies starring the twins, dolls that looked like them, and fashion inspired by them. The Olsens became style icons to young girls!

As the Olsens grew, their senses of style did too. The twins turned their passion for designer clothes into a fashion empire. Today, the Olsens run two successful lines, The Row and Elizabeth and James.

For much of their lives, the Olsens have been fashion trendsetters. Their designs have earned them many awards and a spot among America's top designers.

Ashley (*left*) and Mary-Kate Olsen have won several fashion awards for their clothing brand The Row.

CHILD STARS

Mary-Kate and Ashley Olsen were born on June 13, 1986, in Sherman Oaks, California. They are **sororal** twins. Their parents are Dave, a banker, and Jarnette, a former ballet dancer. Mary-Kate and Ashley have two **siblings** and two half-siblings.

The Olsen twins spent their early years on the set of *Full House*. They were cast on the TV show at just six months old. Casting directors chose the twins because they were friendly and energetic.

Mary-Kate and Ashley also looked enough alike to play the same character. The girls shared the role of Michelle, the youngest daughter on *Full House*. The show began filming in 1987, when the twins were nine months old.

Many Americans liked *Full House*. This was thanks in part to its young stars. Adults and children alike were charmed by

FASHION FACT

Ashley is the older twin by a few minutes.

The twins shared the role of Michelle because rules limited how much time young actors could spend on a set.

Mary-Kate and Ashley's **portrayal** of Michelle. In 1991, a television popularity rating system called TVQ ranked the sisters the second-most likable stars on TV! And as the twins got older, their likability only grew.

OLSEN OBSESSION

American audiences could not get enough of the Olsen twins. Young fans related to the sisters and wanted to see more of them. In 1993, Mary-Kate and Ashley's manager founded the company Dualstar. This became the brand for the Olsens' products.

In following years, the Olsens seemed to be everywhere! Starting in 1994, they starred in a home video series called *The Adventures of Mary-Kate & Ashley*. The twins' first movie in theaters, *It Takes Two*, was released in 1995. That same year, *Full House* ended.

Offscreen, the Olsens' brand continued to soar. Fans read Olsen-inspired books. They played with Olsen dolls. Fans were also eager to imitate the twins' style. When the Olsens wore **bandannas** in one of their movies, kids across the country bought bandannas to match.

The Olsens were fashion trendsetters! In 2001, public interest in the twins' style led the pair to launch a fashion line. They called it mary-kateandashley.

Mary-Kate said starring in movies as a child was as typical as "waking up in the morning and brushing our teeth."

TWEEN SCENE

Mary-Kate and Ashley had lots of fashion experience from their time in Hollywood. On TV and movie sets, the twins were constantly being fitted for outfits. Sometimes they changed clothes 12 times a day!

Television and movie stylists often had items from adult clothing designers cut down and tailored to fit the twins. Through this process, the Olsens learned about fit and gained an appreciation for designer clothes. This helped them develop their own designs.

The mary-kateandashley brand **debuted** in Wal-Mart stores in 2001, when the twins were 14 years old. Products included sportswear, bags, and jewelry. Fans thought the clothes were fashionable and cool, just like the Olsen twins.

The Olsen brand was among the first successful **tween** fashion

FASHION FACT

The mary-kateandashley brand was the first celebrity line ever featured in Wal-Mart stores.

The tagline for mary-kateandashley was "Real Fashion for Real Girls."

lines. By 2002, Olsen-related products, including books, videos, and clothing, had made billions of dollars.

The Olsens' fashion careers were just beginning. In the coming years, the twins would further develop their personal fashion senses. Once again, they would be style trendsetters.

SHABBY & CHIC

In 2004, the Olsen twins left California to go to New York University in New York City. Being famous meant that they were often followed by photographers. These photographers took photos of the twins and sold them to magazines and newspapers. Because of this, the way the Olsens dressed in college became national news.

At the time, it was popular to wear tight-fitting clothes with brand logos. But the Olsen twins wore baggy, oversized clothes without brand names. They mixed high-end and thrift-store pieces to create a luxurious yet shabby look. They also carried **accessories** such as huge, beat-up handbags. One newspaper called the twins' style "dumpster chic."

The Olsens' style once again had people paying attention. Meanwhile, the twins focused on new experiences in college. Mary-Kate **interned** with famous photographer Annie Leibovitz. Ashley interned with famous women's fashion designer Zac Posen.

Mary-Kate (*left*) and Ashley often wore large sunglasses when out in public to help hide their faces from photographers.

In 2005, Mary-Kate decided she wanted to return to movie acting. She dropped out of school and moved back to California. That same year, Ashley also dropped out and moved back to California, but for a different reason.

While in school, Ashley had gotten an idea for a fashion project. She wondered if it would be possible to design the perfect T-shirt. To her, this meant the shirt would fit well and be made with quality fabric. After Ashley left school, she asked her sister to help design a T-shirt like this.

The Olsens spent the next year and a half working on their T-shirt. They tested fabrics and studied patternmaking. They also learned about fashion production.

The twins developed a **prototype** T-shirt in different sizes. Then they had many different people try the prototypes on. This helped the Olsens understand how body type affected fit. Before long, their fashion experiment would inspire a new fashion line!

The Olsens wear loose, muted dresses in 2005. Loose shapes and neutral colors became part of their signature style.

THE ROW

The more the Olsens worked on their T-shirt, the more they saw a need for simple, high-end clothes. So in 2006, they decided to expand their T-shirt into a whole fashion line.

The twins called their new line The Row after Savile Row in London, England. This famous street was known for selling well-tailored men's clothes. Though the Olsen twins were designing for women, they were inspired by the superior fit of Savile Row clothing.

The Row clothing was high-end and meant for adults. Some fashion experts doubted the Olsens could succeed in high fashion. But the twins knew more about fashion than many realized. Though neither sister had formal design training, their years on Hollywood sets gave them practical experience.

FASHION FACT

The Row clothing has been worn by many famous people, including former US First Lady Michelle Obama.

Mary-Kate (*right*) and Ashley wearing The Row clothing

The Olsens also knew a lot about business. Since they were seven, the twins had been involved in decision-making at Dualstar. At eighteen, they became co-presidents of the company. With their experience in style and management, the Olsens were prepared to enter the high-end fashion world.

The Row's first collection was **minimalist**. It featured only seven pieces. One piece was the perfect white T-shirt. There was also a tank top, a dress, leggings, and more. The Olsens wanted their clothing to feel elegant and timeless. One of their goals was to create pieces that customers could pair with clothing from other designers.

The Olsens first sold The Row clothing from a rented hotel room in Paris, France. They made sales one at a time, handwriting individual clothing orders to luxury stores from around the world.

Fashion critics were impressed by The Row's **sophistication**, especially since the Olsens were

IN HER OWN WORDS

"Our clothes are ageless and timeless. They aren't wearing you. You'll be able to wear something a year from now and not be embarrassed you bought it."
—Mary-Kate on
The Row

The Row stores had a minimalist look that reflected the styles of the line's clothing.

younger than most established designers. The critics loved everything from the Olsens' fabric choices to the clothing's details. But as their brand earned recognition, the Olsens tried to stay out of the public eye.

DISCREET DESIGNERS

In their younger years, the Olsens could sell almost any product if it had their names and faces on it. But it was important to them that The Row not be seen as a celebrity fashion line. They wanted the line to sell because it was well made, not because its designers were famous.

The Olsens were often uncomfortable being in the spotlight for their design work. Their names did not appear anywhere on The Row's items. The twins did not model for The Row's photoshoots. And although The Row was on social media, neither twin had an account on any platform.

The Olsens kept The Row's designs **understated**. Its color

IN HER OWN WORDS

"We're not product pushers. I don't know if it's because of the way we grew up—we just don't like talking about ourselves or talking about what we're doing. It's not really our approach."
—Ashley on the Olsens' hope for anonymity as fashion designers

The twins displayed a rare acceptance of public attention for The Row at a 2010 fashion show.

palette often included gray, white, and cream. Some designs featured oversized shapes. Other clothes were slimly cut. No matter the shape, the Olsens took pride in producing well-proportioned clothes.

ELIZABETH AND JAMES

After the Olsens launched The Row, they saw another need in the fashion industry. This time, it was for a casual line that was both luxurious and affordable. In 2007, they founded Elizabeth and James with this vision in mind.

The Olsens were inspired by both menswear and womenswear when creating their new line. They wanted Elizabeth and James to be about balance. Their clothing designs reflected this. The line's tops and dresses were colorful and playful, yet slouchy and sporty.

Vintage clothing was also a huge inspiration for Elizabeth and James' designs. The twins had been collecting vintage clothing for years. Pieces from their collection gave them design ideas.

With another successful fashion line to their names, the Olsen twins were quickly becoming respected fashion figures. The coming years would bring even more fashion projects. The future would also bring the twins recognition for their fashion achievements.

Elizabeth and James are the names of the Olsens' sister and brother. However, the Olsens say their brand is not named after their siblings.

AWARDS & MORE

While the Olsens were running their two fashion lines, they were also working on other projects. In 2008, the twins released *Influence*. It is a book of interviews the sisters conducted asking fashion designers, models, and photographers about their fashion **philosophies**.

The Olsens were also at work on another fashion line. This time, they returned to their roots as teen girls' clothing designers. In 2009, Olsenboye clothing started selling in JCPenney stores nationwide.

Olsenboye sold at JCPenney for years. But it was not as successful as the Olsens' other lines. Some fashion critics found its items expensive and uncomfortable to wear. Meanwhile, the Olsens' other brands were still doing well.

In 2009, the Olsens became the youngest designers ever **inducted** into

FASHION FACT

The name "Olsenboye" comes from the last name the Olsens' Norwegian ancestors used.

Mary-Kate (*right*) said of *Influence*, "Ashley and I interviewed the people who have inspired us, with the hope that they will inspire and teach others."

the Council of Fashion Designers of America (CFDA). In 2012, they won CFDA's Womenswear Designer of the Year award. This is one of the fashion industry's top awards! The Olsens won more CFDA awards, for **accessories** in 2014 and for womenswear in 2015.

FASHION INTO THE FUTURE

The Olsens' fashion careers continued to grow. In 2014, the first The Row store opened in California. The next year, the Olsen family expanded! In November 2015, Mary-Kate married French banker Olivier Sarkozy and became stepmother to his two children.

In 2016, the Olsens opened their first Elizabeth and James store in California. Meanwhile, the twins earned continued recognition. In 2018, they won a second CFDA **Accessories** Designer of the Year Award. It was their fourth CFDA Award.

Later that year, the Olsens expanded The Row to include an official collection of menswear. They took the same detailed approach to this collection as they did with the brand's other items.

The Olsens' **sophisticated** style and attention to detail have made them stars of the fashion industry. Fashion experts are excited to see what the twins will create next. And many critics agree that the Olsens will continue to be style trendsetters in the future!

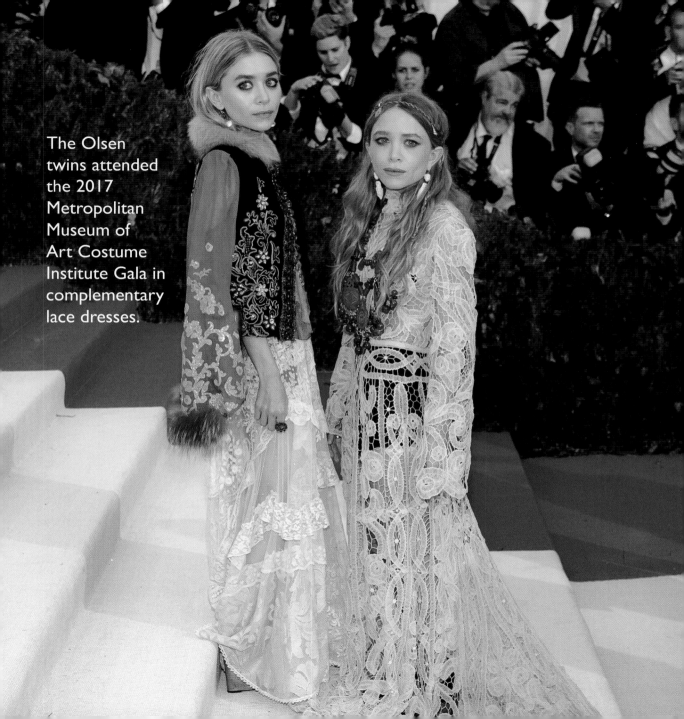

The Olsen twins attended the 2017 Metropolitan Museum of Art Costume Institute Gala in complementary lace dresses.

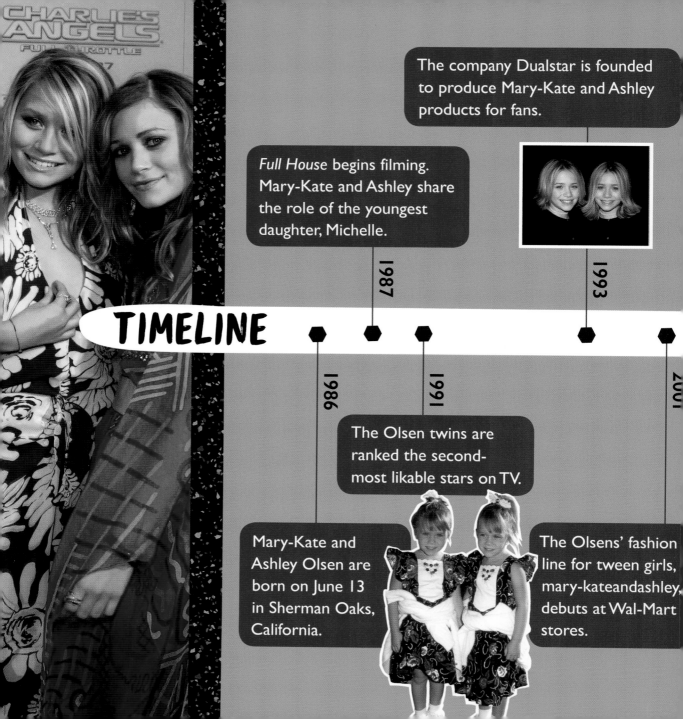

The company Dualstar is founded to produce Mary-Kate and Ashley products for fans.

Full House begins filming. Mary-Kate and Ashley share the role of the youngest daughter, Michelle.

TIMELINE

1987

1993

1986

1991

2001

The Olsen twins are ranked the second-most likable stars on TV.

Mary-Kate and Ashley Olsen are born on June 13 in Sherman Oaks, California.

The Olsens' fashion line for tween girls, mary-kateandashley, debuts at Wal-Mart stores.

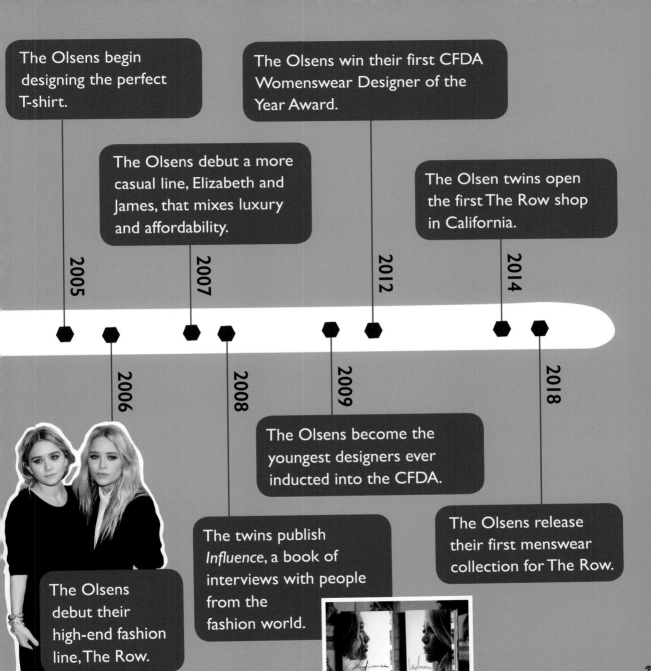

The Olsens begin designing the perfect T-shirt.

The Olsens debut a more casual line, Elizabeth and James, that mixes luxury and affordability.

The Olsens win their first CFDA Womenswear Designer of the Year Award.

The Olsen twins open the first The Row shop in California.

2005

2007

2012

2014

2006

2008

2009

2018

The Olsens become the youngest designers ever inducted into the CFDA.

The twins publish *Influence*, a book of interviews with people from the fashion world.

The Olsens release their first menswear collection for The Row.

The Olsens debut their high-end fashion line, The Row.

GLOSSARY

accessory—a small item that you wear with your clothes, such as a belt, gloves, or a scarf.

bandanna—a large, and often colorfully patterned, handkerchief.

debut—to present or perform something for the first time.

induct—to admit as a member.

intern—to gain practical experience in a professional field by studying under a professional or for an organization.

minimalist—relating to or being as small or revealing as possible.

philosophy (fuh-LAH-suh-fee)—a set of ideas about knowledge and truth.

portrayal—the act of playing a role.

prototype—an early model of a product on which future versions can be modeled.

sibling—a brother or a sister.

sophistication—the quality of having worldly knowledge or experience. Something with this quality is sophisticated.

sororal—relating to twin sisters who may not have the same appearance.

tween—relating to those of the age between a child and a teenager.

understated—without obvious embellishment.

vintage—old but still interesting or of good quality.

ONLINE RESOURCES

Booklinks
NONFICTION NETWORK
FREE! ONLINE NONFICTION RESOURCES

To learn more about Mary-Kate and Ashley Olsen, please visit **abdobooklinks.com** or scan this QR code. These links are routinely monitored and updated to provide the most current information available.

INDEX